BUDGETING MADE EASY

LARRY BURKETT
with BRENDA ARMSTRONG

ISBN 1-56427-083-1

We gratefully acknowledge Gordon Wadsworth's contribution to the development of this book.

All Scripture quotations are taken from the *New American Standard Bible* (updated edition), © 1960, 1962, 1963, 1968, 1971, 1972, 1973, 1975, 1977, 1995 by The Lockman Foundation and are used by permission.

Printed in the United States of America

01-2004

CONTENTS

PROLOGUE

Establishing a budget is sometimes difficult, especially if you have never worked with a budget. It is even more difficult when you don't make enough to cover your basic needs and you have used credit to make up the difference.

If you have a low income or never have worked with a budget, you aren't alone. Many people find it scary to put their finances down on paper. This workbook is designed to help you by providing a step-by-step guide, with worksheets for each category, to help you fill out a one-page budget form. It also gives some tips about some of the problems you may have in working with a budget, getting a bank card, or balancing a checking account.

If you have difficulty working through any part of the workbook, ask someone you trust for help, or write to Crown Financial Ministries and request help from a trained volunteer budget counselor. Volunteer counselors are available around the country to work free of charge with people who need help.

Once you have worked with this budget for six months, you may want to move on to a more complete budget by using *The Financial Planning Workbook*. If you're a single parent, you may want to order *The Financial Guide for the Single Parent* workbook, which includes many money stretching ideas for each budget category. To order either of these resources, call Crown Financial Ministries at 800-722-1976.

We have heard from many people who started using a budget when they had little or no money. The principles they learned helped them overcome their budgeting fears and reduce or pay off their debts. These same principles can change your life.

THE VALUE OF MONEY

In today's society the dollar is king, not because the piece of paper is worth anything. It's not. As a matter of fact, the paper that money is printed on is actually worth almost nothing. What is important is what you believe that those pieces of paper can get you. Money isn't good or bad; it is your attitude about money that can cause you problems. A lot of people believe that money can solve their problems. Maybe you've had similar beliefs.

If I only had more money...

I would get some *respect!*

I could do what *I* want to do!

I could *pay my bills*!

I wouldn't *have to work*!

Everyone would *listen to me*!

I wouldn't feel so much *pressure*!

Most of us have imagined the better life we would have if we only had more money. What have you imagined?

If I had more money I would . . .

———————————————————————

———————————————————————

———————————————————————

It's easy to buy into the idea that if you had lot of money you would be more important or more powerful. You may think that having more money will get you anything you want whenever you want it. Or you may believe that money brings the kind of power that tells people "Don't mess with me!" Since money seems to bring those things, some people have become so obsessed with wanting that kind of power they have risked their families and even their own lives to get it.

Although money may bring power and importance in our society, is the pursuit of money really worth it?

You can't take it with you

King Solomon was one of the richest men that ever lived, but the Bible says he also was considered to be the wisest man who ever lived. Do you know what he thought about all of his wealth? He felt that it was useless because it wasn't eternal. He knew that he couldn't take it with him when he died, so it really didn't amount to anything of any lasting value.

No matter how rich you are, you can't take it with you. John D. Rockefeller, Sr. was one of the richest men in America. When he died, someone asked his bookkeeper, "How much did he leave?" The bookkeeper answered, "Everything."

Wise men know the real value of money. They recognize that we didn't bring anything into this world, and we won't take anything with us when we leave.

Never enough

Those who love money never seem to have enough. Even the rich are not truly happy because money can't buy what they need the most.

God created us for fellowship with Himself and with others. He promised to give us all that we need. He wants us to be content with what He has given us and not go around complaining or comparing ourselves with others. He knows that we are never happy when we are selfish and greedy and always trying to get more for ourselves.

The tightwad

Remember the Christmas story about the stingy rich man named Scrooge? All he cared about was his money. He was selfish and mean and thought Christmas and giving were for fools. Scrooge was going to die a lonely, bitter man if he didn't change his ways.

One night visiting spirits showed Scrooge how selfish his life had been and the doom that awaited him if he didn't change. When he woke up, Scrooge was thrilled to see that he still had time to treat people differently. In the story, Scrooge was given a second chance. His life was changed, and he was happy for the first time, because he had become a giver instead of a taker. Scrooge finally began to understand true wealth, as described in Matthew 6:19-20.

True wealth

"Do not store up for yourselves treasures upon earth, where moth and rust destroy, and where thieves break in and steal. But store up for yourselves treasures in heaven, where neither moth nor rust destroys, and where thieves do not break in or steal" (Matthew 6:19-20).

The riches we lay up in heaven consist of things like love, patience, peace, joy, gentleness, and kindness. These are the things that bring contentment. Only through a relationship with the living God can a person experience these true riches. You may be thinking, *If these are true riches, then what is the purpose of money?*

Our attitude about money

The Bible says a great deal about money. As we mentioned, money is neither good nor bad. The Bible explains that it is the *love* of money that is the root of all evil. It's the craving for money that causes people trouble. Some of us aren't content with what God has given us, even though the Bible tells us that He gives us all that we need.

"And do not seek what you will eat and what you will drink, and do not keep worrying. For all these things the nations of the world eagerly seek; but your Father knows that you need these things. But seek His kingdom, and these things will be added to you" (Luke 12:29-31).

"And my God will supply all your needs according to His riches in glory in Christ Jesus" (Philippians 4:19).

God's gifts

 God cares for our needs—food, clothing, and shelter—by giving each of us talent and the ability to earn an income that will cover our basic needs. The reason so many people suffer in this area is because either they have not tapped into or discovered their talents and abilities or they are stuck in a position that doesn't allow them the opportunity to pursue their gifts and talents.

As a loving Father, God wants to give good gifts to His children. He not only meets our needs, but often He meets our wants and desires. We'll explore the difference in needs, wants, and desires later. The point here is that most of us are not content with just having enough. We want more, or better, than we have.

Giving

It's hard to accept what we have when so many people have more than they need. God doesn't give any of us more so that we can live extravagant lives. He gives us what we need and often gives us more so we can share with others in need.

Having more can become so important that we miss what God wants for us. In Mark 10, Jesus was talking to a rich man who wanted to get into heaven. He was used to buying everything and thought that he could just buy his way in. Jesus could see that money was the most important thing to him, so He told him, *"One thing you lack: go and sell all you possess, and give to the poor, and you will have treasure in heaven; and come, follow Me. But at these words he was saddened, and he went away grieving, for he was one who owned much property"* (Mark 10:21-22).

Would you rather be rich than have eternal life?

Because God loves us, He tells us what might happen if we trust in riches instead of trusting in Him. The Bible says, *"Those who want to get rich fall into temptation and a snare and many foolish and harmful desires which plunge men into ruin and destruction"* (1 Timothy 6:9).

Heavenly bank account

 What we do here on earth is like a deposit in the bank in heaven. That doesn't mean we can buy our way or work our way into heaven; we can receive salvation only through faith—not because of anything we do. Nevertheless, God calls our good deeds riches.

I have met many people who are very rich in spirit but have very few material things. They may be behind on their rent or car payment or maybe not even have a car. Yet, whatever the case, they have found the key to contentment—and it doesn't include lots of money. They have learned to be content no matter what happens to them.

Since God is concerned about all our attitudes, how we think and feel about money is important to Him. We might have a lot of money and things, or we might be totally broke. Only our attitudes about money will affect our personal relationship with Him—not how much or how little we have.

Trust in God

Christians are called to trust God, no matter what. Many times we must still suffer the consequences for our bad decisions, including the financial ones. But we can trust God to help us in every situation, when we put our faith and trust in Him and not in ourselves. That means we must trust Him with everything: our families, where we live, what we eat, or paying the rent and the phone bill.

In the prison ministries we hear people say, "Hey, I tried the straight and narrow and it didn't work. I can make more money on the streets."

Welfare families say, "I'll just stay on the state and I won't have to worry about a car or job."

Others who are really trying say, "I'm doing all I can, and I just can't get ahead. What's the use? God doesn't care."

God gets our attention

God may allow us to go through some very rough times to get our attention. We often see that in prison ministries. One minister told us about an inmate named Robert that he met at a prison Bible study. Robert had been convicted of several charges and was facing a lot of prison time.

Before prison, Robert never went to church. He was

involved with the wrong crowd and got into a lot of trouble. However, while he was in jail awaiting sentencing, he heard about how he could be free in Jesus Christ. Although many of the prisoners gave the minister a hard time, he returned night after night and Robert listened. God had captured his attention, and it was there in that jail cell that Robert committed his life to Jesus Christ.

Robert told everyone that he was thankful he had been sent to prison. Over the next few weeks the preacher watched Robert to see if his commitment was real. Week after week Robert would come bouncing into the Bible study with a bright smile on his face—except for one night. It was obvious he was troubled. The group prayed for him, and that was the last time they ever saw him.

They later heard that security had gone to his cell in the middle of the night and shipped him out to a distant city. Apparently there was a contract out on him; someone wanted to kill him.

The minister said that he would never forget Robert. He really was pleased that God was making such a change in his life, and he felt certain that Robert had learned to trust in God for everything . . . including his life!

Is it easy to trust God like that? No way! It's hard to trust God when your kids are sick, or the refrigerator is empty, or you don't even have enough money to ride the bus. It seems a lot easier to trust the money in your pockets, doesn't it? And yet the Bible says that God wants you to have faith in Him to bless you with everything you need to enjoy life. Do you have that kind of faith?

The good news

God wants you to know peace. He wants to be the One—the only One—you put your trust in. It's easy to trust in something you can see. It's harder to trust in something you can't see, even though you do it all the time. You trust that the air you breathe will be there to keep you alive. You don't even stop to think about it. That's the kind of trust you have to have in God to obtain the peace He wants to give you. You have to believe that He cares for you and that He is providing for you even when you can't see it.

What are you afraid of?

Maybe your fears and frustrations are keeping you from trusting God. Before you go any further, take a few minutes to write down all the fears and frustrations that you are dealing with right now.

_____

_____

_____

_____

_____

_____

The answer

Because He loves you, God wants the best for you. He wants you to trust Him for everything. And because He is patient, He'll help you take a step of faith and turn all of these concerns over to Him.

You may not know it, but God began providing for you long before you were ever born. He saw that people would sin and that they would need a Savior to redeem them. That's why He sent Jesus. Jesus paid for your sins on a cross a long time ago. Although Jesus died on that cross, God raised Him from the dead, and now He sits right beside God in heaven, praying for you. All you have to do to receive the peace He provided for you is to believe in Him and His sacrifice for you.

If you would like to turn your life and all your frustrations over to God, then pray a prayer similar to this one.

Dear Father God, I want my life to be different. I realize there are things that are more important than money. I want to learn to put my trust in You for all my needs. Thank you for sending your son Jesus to die for my sins. I receive that gift of salvation. Thank you for making me part of the family of God. Now, take my life, and make something beautiful out of it.

Be careful

Even after you've turned your life over to God, you need to be careful. Satan is just around the corner with another get-rich-quick scheme, a lottery ticket, or a great deal that will steal your trust away from God. Satan's goal is to have you trust in yourself and in money. This is the most important decision you will ever make. If you prayed that prayer, write down the date and time that you made this commitment, so you can remember it when the going gets tough.

I accepted God's gift of salvation on _____

Sign your name _____

FINANCIAL BONDAGE

What comes to your mind when you think of bondage? I think of someone tied up with no way to escape. Did you ever play cowboys and Indians as a child? Usually children take turns, pretending to shoot at each other or hide. Sometimes they sneak up behind another child and "capture" him or her. Once caught, the "prisoner" is tied to a tree in the yard until someone lets him or her go.

Even though it was part of the game, I didn't like being the one that was tied to the tree. It was kind of scary. I could hardly move and was trapped until someone came to rescue me.

Being in financial bondage makes you feel the same way. It sneaks up on you and there seems to be no way out—no way of escape. You feel trapped. Years ago, when people didn't pay their bills they were thrown into a "debtor's prison," and their families became slaves to the person they owed the money to.

A different kind of prison

Today, you no longer face going to jail for not paying your debts, but there is a prison that can hold you captive. That prison's bars are made up of worry, fear, and frustration, and it holds you captive emotionally, spiritually, physically, and mentally.

Are you in financial bondage?

If you're in financial bondage, then you probably are experiencing some of the following signs. Place a check by the ones that are causing you problems.

- ❏ You're afraid to answer the phone or door, because it might be a debt collector.
- ❏ You feel tremendous guilt, because you've made promises to pay that you can't keep.
- ❏ You blow up over small things.
- ❏ You are constantly worried.
- ❏ You overspend when you have money to "relieve the pressure."
- ❏ You blame others.
- ❏ You avoid family or friends who have loaned you money, because you can't repay them.

Overcoming debt

God doesn't want us to be in debt. The Bible says that only the wicked person borrows and does not repay (see Psalm 37:21). It also says that the poor are ruled by the rich, and those who borrow are slaves of lenders (see Proverbs 22:7).

Easy credit

Unfortunately, our society doesn't see it that way. Credit cards are issued too easily today. College students with no income can get credit cards easily.

One college student used to brag to his friends about all the credit cards he had acquired before his 20th birthday. He took great pleasure in pulling out his cardholder, which held 28 plastic cards that unfolded like an accordion. He used them to impress his friends, buying things he couldn't afford. He ran up large debts and used one card to pay another. Without realizing it, he had become a slave to the credit card companies.

A single mother who needed a car bought into the

idea that she could buy her car at one of those "buy here, pay here" places that guarantee that no one will be turned down for credit. She bought an older model car and discovered that she would be paying double what the car was worth in high interest. After she bought the car the engine blew, and she was left with a huge car debt and no car.

Finding financial freedom

It is not always a lack of money or too much money that puts financial pressure on us. Many times it is simply a matter of attitude. If our attitude toward money is right, we can be free of the bondage that might entrap us.

It surprises many people to find that approximately two-thirds of all the stories that Jesus told in the Bible deal with money. The reason is simple: Jesus chose a topic that everyone could identify with, whether young or old, rich or poor. Everyone can relate to money.

Keep in mind that God did not say that money and material things are (in themselves) a problem. As we discussed previously, money is neither good nor bad. It is the *use* of it and your attitude toward it that is important. Therefore, we should guard our hearts against greed and pride. These are the tools that Satan uses to control and manipulate us!

Eight steps to financial freedom

Step 1. Transfer Ownership

God has put the most difficult step at the front. God wants you to transfer ownership of all you have to Him. What does it mean to transfer ownership? Since you can't literally hand it to God, it is simply an act of faith. It means accepting the fact that God owns it all anyway.

Transferring ownership to God also means that God has the right to tell you what to do with your clothes, your car, your home, your family, your future and, most important, your paycheck. Oh yes, all your debts too. Once you give up ownership of everything in your life, God can begin to lead you out of debt and into freedom from the frustration and worry that once imprisoned you.

God wants it all. If I left anything out, add that to your list. If you believe that you are the owner of even *one item*, it's going to affect your attitude.

If God is the owner of everything in your life, you can trust Him to change your buying habits. If you have a problem with impulse spending, develop a new set of standards. Making a spending plan for impulse items can free you from overspending, especially with credit cards!

It is not an easy thing to tell God that He now owns everything we thought we owned. God won't force us to transfer ownership, but when we do He'll keep His promise to provide every need we have. *Financial freedom comes from knowing that God is in complete control.*

Step 2. Get Out of Debt

There are many ways to get in debt other than credit cards. One that is the most dangerous is the new car trap. Others include a desire for a bigger house, better furniture, surround-sound stereo, or maybe name brand clothes or shoes. Here are some tips that will help you stay focused on remaining debt-free.

- Develop a written plan of all the things you want to buy. Determine whether the expense or purchase is because of a need, a want, or a desire.

The following will help to illustrate the difference.

Needs — necessities like food, clothing, housing, or medical care.

Wants — things that make life a little easier or more comfortable: a microwave oven, a VCR, or air conditioning.

Desires — more expensive things: designer clothes, name brand shoes, a new BMW, or a wide-screen TV.

- Open a savings account and get in the habit of putting something into your savings account every week, regardless of how small the amount. You may want to establish a "goal" for your savings account like a vacation, a gift, a new car, or maybe even for that unexpected repair bill. *"A faithful man will abound with blessings, but he who makes haste to be rich will not go unpunished"* (Proverbs 28:20).

Step 3. Establish a Tithe

Every Christian should give something back to God as a testimony to God's ownership. A tithe is the portion of our income that we give to God. Tithe means "tenth." This is the amount most people use as a guide for beginning to tithe. If you are part of a church, your tithe belongs there. If you're not able to attend church, then you can give your tithe to a Christian fellowship, ministry, or organization that you feel is worthy. In every case, God wants us to give the first part to Him. *"Honor the Lord from your wealth, and from the first of all your produce"* (Proverbs 3:9).

Step 4. Accept What God Provides

We are expected to live on what God provides and not to be pressured by the desire for riches and material things.

In the Bible, the apostle Paul wrote about how he learned to be content with what God had given him. He was determined that he was not going to complain about having too little. He was satisfied with whatever God gave him. Paul knew what it was like to be poor, and he knew what it was like to have plenty, because he had lived under all kinds of conditions. He knew what it meant to be full and to be hungry, to have too much and too little. He learned that the strength to face his struggles came from God (see Philippians 4:11).

Step 5. Put Others First

It is not God's plan for us to get ahead at someone else's expense. We must keep others' needs in mind. *"Do not neglect doing good and sharing, for with such sacrifices God is pleased"* (Hebrews 13:16).

Step 6. Avoid Indulgence

To achieve financial freedom, we should avoid spending more than we can afford on things that we don't really need. Indulgence is greed. *"Immorality or any impurity or greed must not be named among you, as is proper among saints"* (Ephesians 5:3).

Step 7. Avoid Snap Decisions

Avoid impulse spending, get-rich-quick schemes, and other fast decisions. The best way to do this is to pray about each purchase and every opportunity that you might have to earn extra income. *"Rest in the Lord and wait patiently for Him; do not fret because of him who prospers in his way, because of the man who carries out wicked schemes"* (Psalm 37:7).

Step 8. Seek Wise Counsel

Look for people who can give you counsel on important matters. Without good advice, everything goes wrong. It takes careful planning for things to go right. *"A wise man will hear and increase in learning, and a man of understanding will acquire wise counsel"* (Proverbs 1:5).

FINANCIAL FREEDOM

The plan

 Many people ask the same question, "Do I really need a plan?" The answer is always the same: Yes! A budget, or spending plan, will help anyone, regardless of how much or how little he or she has.

The best reason for having a spending plan is because it helps you see where your money is coming from and where your money is going.

A budget is not intended to be a ball and chain, so you no longer have any fun. Instead, it's a way for you to see the choices you can make *before* you end up having to live with the consequences of bad decisions.

A budget can help you see where you may be spending too much money. It also can let you see where you need to have more money in order to cover your expenses. And finally, a well-planned budget or spending plan can help you get out of debt.

A spending plan is like a road map. It not only helps you see where you are going, it also helps you see where you've already been. You wouldn't plan a long trip without a map, so why try to handle your money without some kind of guide to help you?

The cash system

There are many different ways to keep track of your money. It is not important which method you use. It is more important that you use the kind of plan that helps you manage your money, rather than letting the money manage you.

If you feel more comfortable keeping your money in cash, you may want to try the envelope system. Here's how it works.

- Mark a different envelope for each monthly expense, such as Food, Rent, Utilities, Car Payment, or Transportation.

- Write the amount you need for the month on the envelope.

- Write the due date on the envelope.

- Put the money you need to pay each bill in the appropriate envelope.

- When the bill is due, go to the store and buy a money order in that amount to mail the payment, or pay the bill in person.

- Remember to keep envelopes for bills that are not due every month, such as Insurance.

Crown Financial Ministries has created a *Cash Organizer* that you can use with the envelope system to manage your money. A *Bill Organizer* is also available to help organize expenses.

Write your plan

Whether you're using cash or a checking account, you need a written plan. In the next section we'll begin by looking at what you're already spending. Make two copies of the following Budget Guide to get started. Mark one copy "Current Budget" and mark the other copy "New Budget." Use the worksheets on the following pages to see how to fill in your forms.

You may not be spending in all the categories listed, and you probably will need to change some areas to fit your particular situation.

BUDGET GUIDE

A. Income (see worksheet) $ _____

B. Monthly Expenses

    1. Tithe $ _____

    2. Child support/alimony $ _____

    3. Housing $ _____

    4. Food $ _____

    5. Clothing $ _____

    6. Transportation $ _____

    7. Entertainment $ _____

    8. Miscellaneous $ _____

    9. Savings $ _____

    10. Medical care $ _____

    11. Debt $ _____

    12. Life insurance $ _____

    13. Child care $ _____

       Total $ _____

C. The Difference

Total Income $ _____

Total Monthly Expenses $ _____

Amount over or under what is needed $ _____

Fill out the "Current Budget" sheet first with the amounts you are currently receiving and paying. You will fill in the "New Budget" sheet after you decide where adjustments can be made in each category. If you need help, ask someone you trust to help you. Let's start with income.

A. Income

This category includes any type of money you receive each month. Use the following worksheet to help you fill in your current income.

List the amount of money you *receive* from each of the following sources.

$ _____   Take-home pay from work (after taxes are deducted)

$ _____   Self-employment income*

$ _____   Tips, bonuses

$ _____   Welfare

$ _____   Social Security

$ _____   Disability

$ _____   Worker's compensation

$ _____   Unemployment

$ _____   Child support

$ _____   Alimony

$ _____   Insurance or trust

$ _____   Food stamp allotment

$ _____   Other _____

$ _____   Total

*If you are self-employed, be sure to subtract the amount you need to pay self-employment taxes from the amount you earn each month.

Place the total amount of income in the space provided on the Budget Guide. When filling out your "New Budget" sheet, create your budget based on income that you are certain you will receive. For example, if you are currently receiving alimony and it will end soon, don't include that amount on your new budget sheet. Likewise, if you're currently receiving child support and there's a possibility that you will not be able to count on it, then don't include that amount.

B. *Monthly Expenses*

These categories are expenses you pay every month and the expenses you pay periodically. We'll look at each category individually so you can accurately evaluate your expenses. Don't try to figure your new budget yet. Just write what you are currently paying in each area.

1. **Tithe:** Fill in the dollar amount you are giving each month. If you are not tithing now, leave that line blank.

2. **Child support:** If you are required to pay child support, enter the amount you are required to pay per month. Most court orders are based on weekly amounts; to figure your monthly amount fill in the following.

$ _____ Weekly amount paid in child support

_____ **X 52**

= _____ Amount paid per year

Amount paid per year $ _____ divided by 12 =

$ _____

Place your answer on the **Child Support** line.

3. **Housing costs:** Use the following worksheet to figure your total monthly Housing expense.

Fill in the amounts you have to pay each month. For payments that change from month to month, like gas or electric, figure an average payment by adding three high monthly bills together and dividing the total by three. For payments that you only pay once a year, such as Taxes or Insurance, divide the amount you pay each year by 12 for a monthly amount.

$ _____   Rent or mortgage

$ _____   Taxes

$ _____   Home or renter's insurance

$ _____   Gas/fuel oil

$ _____   Electric

$ _____   Water

$ _____   Trash

$ _____   Telephone

$ _____   Maintenance

$ _____   Other

$ _____   Total

Enter your total amount in the housing category on your **"Current Budget"** sheet.

4. **Food:** This category includes all the food and beverages you buy at the grocery store, including pet food. Do not include take-out food or eating out expenses. Those go under Entertainment.

If you receive food stamps, use the following worksheet to figure your expenses. Enter the amount in dollars of food stamps you receive. Then enter the amount you actually spend in cash each month to supplement the food stamps.

$ _____ Food stamps

$ _____ Cash spent on food and other grocery store items

$ _____ Total spent at the grocery for one month

Enter the total on the **Food** category line.

5. **Clothing:** Since this is not a monthly expense, it is hard to estimate a monthly amount. If you keep receipts, add the amounts you spent on all of the families' clothing for the last three months. Divide your answer by three for a monthly amount. For a more accurate figure, use a three-month period when you buy a lot of clothes, such as before school or at Christmas.

For example:		Your estimate:	
$ __32.00__ July		$ _____ Month _____	
$ __72.00__ Aug.		$ _____ Month _____	
$ __38.00__ Sept.		$ _____ Month _____	
$ __142.00__ Total		$ _____ Total	

$142 divided by 3 = $47.33   Total $_____ divided by 3

=_____

Your answer goes on the **Clothing** category line.

6. **Transportation:** Use the following worksheet. Fill out all that you pay on Transportation. Many of these expenses vary, so you will need to figure your monthly amount by adding several months expenses together, like you did for the Clothing category, and then divide by the number of months you included. For the Insurance amount, if you pay every six months, take the total amount you pay and divide by six. If you pay monthly, just enter that amount. If you don't currently have insurance, leave that line blank.

$ _____ Car payment

$ _____ Car insurance

$ _____ Gas and oil or oil changes

$ _____ Car repairs

$ _____ Car replacement fund

$ _____ Bus fare or subway tokens

$ _____ Parking

$ _____ Other

$ _____ Total

Enter the total on the line for **Transportation.**

7. **Entertainment:** This category includes eating out. Use the following worksheet to figure your monthly entertainment expenses.

If you go on vacation only once a year, divide the amount you spend by 12. If you go to events only once in a while, figure how much you spend each year and divide by 12.

$ _____ Eating out

$ _____ Movies (rental or theater)

$ _____ Cable TV

$ _____ Sports events

$ _____ Vacation

$ _____ Concerts

$ _____ Other

$ _____ Total

Enter the total on the **Entertainment** line.

8. **Miscellaneous:** This category includes every-thing not listed in any other category, such as cleaning supplies, health and beauty products, hair cuts, and laundry expenses.

   Divide the cost of products or services by the number of months between purchases. For items purchased weekly, multiply the cost of the items by 52 and divide your answer by 12. Use the following example to get started.

Item	Cost	How often purchased	Monthly Amt
Laundry soap	$4.99	every two months	2.50
Laundromat	$5.00	every week	22.00
Bath soap	$3.00	6 bars/ two months	1.50
Furniture polish	$2.99	every six months	.50

   Add all of your miscellaneous monthly amounts and place the total on the **Miscellaneous** line.

9. **Savings:** Enter only the amount you are currently saving. Since you are working with your income after taxes and deductions, do not include any savings or retirement plans that are automatically deducted from your pay. (See "Income," page 22.)

10. **Medical Care:** This category includes doctor and dentist visits, prescriptions, health insurance premiums or deductibles, and testing expenses that you pay. It does not include charges covered by any other source, such as Medicaid, Medicare, insurance, Social Security, or disability. Do not include any expenses that are reimbursed to you through a tax-free medical savings plan at work.

    Remember to figure amounts on a monthly basis. For example, if you paid for a family member to have a tooth extracted, none of the charge was allowed in your health plan, and you were not reimbursed through a medical savings plan, then you divide the full amount you paid by 12 for a monthly amount.

11. **Debt:** This category includes all of your current monthly payments on credit cards, loans, and purchases, such as appliances or furniture. Enter the total amount you owe monthly on the debt line. If you have a debt that you do not pay monthly, then divide the amount you owe for one year by 12 for a monthly amount.

12. **Life insurance:** Fill in this category if you pay life insurance premiums on yourself or another family member. If premiums are paid monthly enter that amount.

13. **Child care:** Fill in this category if you pay some-one to care for your children while you work. If you pay a weekly amount, multiply the amount by 52; then divide your answer by 12 to get the monthly amount.

C. *The Difference*

At the bottom of your "Current Expenses" form, in the place marked Total Income, place the figure you listed at the top of the form.

Next, enter the total amount of your monthly expenses.

Then, subtract the monthly expenses from your income. You should have a plus or minus amount as a result.

If you have a plus, you are currently meeting your monthly expenses and may only need to adjust your budget to include some missing categories.

If you have a minus, you are not making enough to meet your monthly expenses and will need to make some decisions about each category of spending.

THE NEW SPENDING PLAN

Now it's time to start working on your new budget—your spending plan. Normally this is done with the help of a Percentage Guideline. However, the amount that people spend for each category varies widely so we will not use a Percentage Guideline.

For example, one family may live in subsidized housing and only pay a few dollars a month on Housing, well below the average 35 percent. Another family may be paying a rent of $450 a month, but with all of the housing costs included they may be spending over 60 percent of their income on Housing.

Both of these families can have budgets that work. However, they must adjust other categories to do so. A family in subsidized housing will need to keep other expenses low, because as their income rises so does their rent. A family paying $450 a month rent could cover their expenses if they don't have any car payments and only carry liability insurance on their car or use public transportation.

The key

The key is to adjust your spending so that all of your expenses are covered by your monthly income. If you have trouble figuring out where you can adjust, you may need to work with someone trained in budget counseling, such as one of the volunteer referral counselors trained by Crown Financial Ministries.

Budget Busters

Credit cards

Credit cards are a major budget buster for many people. It is hard to resist the temptation to use credit when so many places are making their cards available. Credit used to be harder to get. Most people only had one or two credit cards, usually a credit card from a bank and a gas card. Now, everyone is offering credit: banks, gas stations, credit unions, discount stores, department stores, the phone company, repair shops, tire stores—you name it and there's a card for it. Many of them tempt you with free gifts or special discounts on your purchase when you sign up.

 No one doubts that the credit card is an incredible advance in the area of finances. No matter where you are in the world, you can buy anything simply by showing your credit card and *paying for it later.* Not only is it easy, it's convenient. You don't have to have money to buy whatever you want or need.

Like money, credit cards are not bad. Problems come when you don't use them correctly. The only time a credit card is of any real benefit is when you only buy what you have planned in your budget and you're able to pay the full amount each month. The following are a few things you should know about credit cards.

- Interest rates on credit cards vary a great deal.

- Department store credit cards usually charge the highest interest.

- Most cards that advertise a low interest rate will allow the low rate only for a limited time or for transferring balances from another card.

- Although most cards have an "interest-free" grace period, most people pay interest because they pay the minimum amount instead of the *full amount* owed each month by the due date.

- Although you may not pay an annual fee, most banks charge a minimum service charge for your use of the cards.

Cash withdrawals

If interest on credit cards isn't bad enough, the creators of these cards have provided other ways for you to get in trouble: cash withdrawals. What could be easier than putting a plastic card in a machine and suddenly receiving $100? When you use the credit card to withdraw cash, the bank normally charges an immediate service charge, plus interest from the day you withdrew the money.

The cost

The average person pays a $20 annual fee for a major credit card and has a balance of $1,000 charged on the card. Using an interest rate of 19.8 percent, if a person pays only the minimum amount each month and *never charges again*, it will take over eight (8) years to pay back the $1,000. In addition, when all the interest and annual fees are added, that person will end up paying a total of $2,023 *for the privilege* of charging $1,000 on their credit card![1]

You can see by the above example that a credit card does not allow you to buy more. It actually allows you to buy less. By the time you pay all the finance charges, you will have less money to spend in the long run. Therefore, it doesn't matter which credit card you have, **if you do not have the money in the bank to pay the total amount of the bill when it arrives, do not use the card.**

Getting Rid of Credit Card Debt

If you already have a problem with credit card debt, don't think that it's hopeless. We've heard many testimonies about people who made up their minds to become debt-free and succeeded. Start with the following suggestions.

1. Stop using your cards. Cut them up. This is critical. If you don't have any credit cards you won't be tempted to overspend.

2. Work out a pay-back plan with the credit card companies. Most credit card companies are eager to develop a repayment plan instead of turning your debt over to a collection agency. You must stick to your agreement or they can make your life fairly miserable.

3. Ask for a reduction in the amount of interest, based on your plan to pay them *promptly*.

4. Purchase on a cash-only basis. In other words, only spend money you have. Even more important, only spend money you have in your spending plan. (Review Chapter 3.)

There are organizations, such as Consumer Credit Counseling Services, available in most cities that can help you work out pay-back plans for your debts, often at no additional interest. Services are usually free. However, you must follow the plan exactly or your creditors will demand the full amount owed.

It is very easy to get into debt. It is very *hard* to get out of debt. However, if you follow the four points mentioned above, you will soon become free of the financial slavery that credit card debt produces.

No Payments – No Interest

You've seen the ads, "no payments, no interest for six months" or "no interest for a full year." If it sounds too good to be true, usually it is. Even if the item you're buying is on sale for a great price, you could end up paying a lot more than the item is worth through some of these payment arrangements.

When you purchase an item through one of these plans, you are actually applying for a credit card from the store. The terms are usually in fine print and not easy to understand. The following may help you decide if you can afford these "deals."

- If you pay the full amount due before the grace period ends, you will pay no interest.

- In the "no interest, no payments" deals, if you don't make any payments during the six-month to one-year grace period, interest will be due when payments begin.

- In the "no interest" deals, if you do not pay the full amount by the time the grace period ends, you still will owe interest on the full amount of the purchase.

Example: if you bought a refrigerator for $600 on a "six months same as cash" deal and you made monthly payments of $100, you would not owe any interest or payments at the end of the six-month grace period.

However, if you paid the minimum monthly amount, about $40, on time every month, you would have a balance of $360 at the end of the six-month grace period, and you wouldn't owe just $360 plus interest on the balance, you would owe $360 plus interest on the entire $600 purchase.

Bad Credit? No Problem

Many people have fallen victim to companies that give them credit when no one else will, whether it's a furniture store, a clothing store, a rent-to-own operation, an appliance store, or a used car lot that advertises, "buy here – pay here." This easy credit comes at a high price. Buyers always spend much more than the products are worth, in sales price and in interest. Then, loan sharks come along to rescue those who have gotten in over their heads with consolidation loans and easy-payment loans, which add interest on top of interest.

Why do these companies give credit to people who are considered poor credit risks? High interest rates and instant repossession policies are only two of the reasons. Many years ago the writer of the Proverbs in the Bible warned us about such dealings. *"The naive believes everything, but the sensible man considers his steps"* (Proverbs 14:15).

Checking Accounts

A checking account is a good way to keep track of your expenses, but it is not for everyone. Some people have a difficult time understanding and balancing a checking account; others just prefer using cash. People without checking accounts often use an envelope system similar to the one described on pages 18 and 19 to organize their money.

If you have never used a checking account, but would like to, the following information will help you.

Opening an account

Banks require a cash deposit to open an account. The amount of the deposit varies. You may open a savings account and a checking account at the same time, or you may just open one account. Most checking accounts will have a monthly fee, which is automatically deducted from your account. Some accounts don't charge a monthly fee if you keep a certain balance. These balance amounts are usually pretty high, so you probably should plan on paying a monthly fee.

In addition to monthly fees, you will be charged for check or draft printing. Other fees might include making more deposits or withdrawals than your bank allows each month or using an Automatic Teller Machine (ATM) card. Be sure you understand all the fees you may be charged so that you don't get in trouble with your account.

Bounced checks

A check or draft is considered a *debit* on your account. That means that when the bank receives the check it is automatically deducted from your balance. If you do not have enough money in your account when you write a check or withdraw money, you will cause an "overdraft," or "bounced check."

When a check bounces, the bank will send the check back to the store as a bad check. The store will send it to the bank again for payment. If there's not enough money in the account, the bank will return the check to the store again. By the time you receive notice that the check was bad, it may have "bounced" back and forth between the store and the bank three times! Your name gets added to a bad-checks list, and the store will no longer accept checks from you.

You have to pay the original amount of your purchase to the store in cash and pay the store a large fee for handling a bad check. The bank will also charge you a fee each time the check is received for payment.

This can cause serious problems. For example, if you bought an item for $2.50 and the check bounced, your purchase could cost you $77.50 or more, as shown in the following example.

$ 2.50   purchase

$20.00   bank fee for overdraft

$35.00   store charge for overdraft

<u>$20.00</u>   <u>second bank charge</u>

$77.50   Total

While this bouncing was going on, other checks that you thought were covered could bounce due to automatic charges. One way to avoid bounced checks is to make a habit of recording every check in your checkbook register when you write the check and do not write checks when the funds are not there.

Writing a check

Writing a check is pretty easy. Just fill in the blanks.

SARA SMITH 4218 SUNRISE DR. SEASIDE, CA 90021	562 DATE *10-30-97*
P_{AY TO THE} _{ORDER OF} *Glenbury Apts*	$ 150.00
One hundred fifty and ^{no}/100	DOLLARS
CITY BANK	
FOR *Deposit* *Sara Smith*	
:073 706 9032:	

- Fill in the correct date.

- Write the name of the company or person the check is to on the top line.

- Fill in the amount of the check in numbers at the end of the first line.

- Write out the number on the second line.

- Sign the check on the "signature" line at the bottom right.

- If you're paying a bill, write the account number on the line at the bottom left of the check.

Keeping it straight

NUMBER	DATE	CODE	DESCRIPTION OF TRANSACTION	PAYMENT/DEBIT(-)		FEE	TAX	DEPOSIT/CREDIT(+)		$ BALANCE	
561	10/15		Sears	12	95					32	48
	10/18		Paycheck					232	00	264	48
562	10/30		Glenbury Apts	150	00					114	48
	11/2		debit-BP Gas	12	00					102	48

Your checkbook will come with a register (ledger) for you to keep track of the checks you've written. As mentioned, you need to write down every check you write or every withdrawal you make immediately and subtract it from your balance. When you put money into your account, add it to your balance.

ATM cards

Many people use Automatic Teller Machine (ATM) cards to make purchases or withdraw cash. These cards are also called "debit" cards, because each withdrawal or charge is automatically deducted from your checking or savings account. These cards are very convenient, because many stores and gas stations accept them and you don't have to carry around a lot of cash. However, there are a few very important things you should keep in mind when using a debit card.

1. Don't rely on the balance you get from the ATM machine. The machine does not know about the checks you've written that have not cleared the bank.

2. In your checkbook register, write down every amount at the time that you use the card. Save every receipt so that you can verify what you've written.

3. Don't use part of your Social Security number for a PIN number. Memorize your PIN number; do not carry it with you.

4. If the card is lost or stolen, report it immediately.

Visa and MasterCard Check Cards

These cards are not credit cards, they are actually debit cards that are accepted at more places. You do not charge your purchases. You have to have money in your account to cover each use. You can use them at any ATM or business that allows debit card purchases. However, since the cards look like Visa® or MasterCard® credit cards, they also can be used anywhere credit cards are accepted, including stores that would normally refuse a check.

For many people, a check card is better than a credit card. When you use a check card, the merchant will process your purchase as if you had a regular credit card, but instead of charging the purchase to you and adding interest the bank deducts the money directly from your bank account. These cards are easy to use, but there are some things you should know before using a check card.

1. You can only use a check card if you have money in the bank to back it up. Although the merchant runs the check card through the bank automatically, the balance the bank is using may not be accurate, especially if you still have checks that have not cleared. Be sure that the balance in your checkbook register shows enough funds to cover the purchase. Better yet, don't spend any amount that you have not planned for in your budget.

2. Like ATM cards, you must record every use of the check card immediately. Receipts are easy to lose.

3. Be sure that you balance your checkbook each month and keep track of all your check card purchases. If you overdraw your account, the bank has stiff penalties.

Lost or stolen cards

Although bank cards are convenient, there are some risks.

1. If the bank card is lost or stolen and you report it within 48 hours, the bank will hold you responsible for only up to $50 worth of charges.

2. If you do not report the loss within the first 48 hours, you can be held responsible for up to $500 worth of charges.

Balancing a Checkbook

Each month, the bank will send you a statement that shows its record of your account. It is amazing how many people don't take the time to balance their checkbooks. It is not that difficult, and it is the only way you're going to find out whether you or the bank made a mistake. It is important that you compare the figures you have in your checkbook register against the bank statement to see if you both agree. The following steps will help you balance your checkbook.

1. **Cleared checks:** For each check listed on the bank statement, find the corresponding check listed in your checkbook register and place a mark beside it. Then mark the check off on your bank statement.

2. **Deposits:** For each deposit listed on the bank statement, find the corresponding deposit listed in your checkbook register and place a mark beside it. Then mark the deposit off on your bank statement.

3. **Withdrawals:** For each withdrawal from the bank or ATM listed on the bank statement, find the corresponding withdrawal listed in your checkbook register and place a mark beside it. Then mark the withdrawal off on your bank statement.

4. **ATM purchases:** For each ATM purchase listed on the bank statement, find the corresponding ATM purchase listed in your checkbook register and place a mark beside it. Then mark the ATM purchase off on your bank statement.

5. **Fees:** Verify each fee listed on the bank statement. If you have not already written the fees in your checkbook register, do so and subtract them from your current balance. Since the bank has already deducted the fees, mark them off the statement and in your checkbook register.

6. **Deposits not listed:** If there are any deposits listed in your checkbook register that are not on the bank statement, add them to the balance shown on your bank statement.

7. **Withdrawals not listed:** On the back of your bank statement, write the amount of any checks, withdrawals, or ATM purchases listed in your checkbook that were not listed on the bank statement. These items have not yet cleared the bank. Subtract these items from the amount you came up with in step six.

8. The answer from step seven should match the balance in your checkbook register. If it does, you are finished. If it doesn't match, try adding the numbers again. If you still cannot get your checkbook register to balance with the statement, ask your bank for help.

Freedom

After you have decided which areas of your current budget can be changed, fill in the New Budget form with your adjusted figures. This new budget should be flexible. If you keep your budget up-to-date, keep track of your spending, spend only what you have, and avoid debt, you will find financial freedom!

---

1. *The Ultimate Credit Handbook,* Gerri Detweiler, Plume Publishing, 1993, p.55

BUDGET GUIDE

A. Income (see worksheet) $ _____

B. Monthly Expenses

    1.   Tithe $ _____

    2.   Child support/alimony $ _____

    3.   Housing $ _____

    4.   Food $ _____

    5.   Clothing $ _____

    6.   Transportation $ _____

    7.   Entertainment $ _____

    8.   Miscellaneous $ _____

    9.   Savings $ _____

  10. Medical care $ _____

  11. Debt $ _____

  12. Life insurance $ _____

  13. Child care $ _____

        Total $ _____

C. The Difference

Total Income $ _____

Total Monthly Expenses $ _____

Amount over or under what is needed $ _____

BUDGET GUIDE

A. Income (see worksheet) $ _____

B. Monthly Expenses

1. Tithe $ _____

2. Child support/alimony $ _____

3. Housing $ _____

4. Food $ _____

5. Clothing $ _____

6. Transportation $ _____

7. Entertainment $ _____

8. Miscellaneous $ _____

9. Savings $ _____

10. Medical care $ _____

11. Debt $ _____

12. Life insurance $ _____

13. Child care $ _____

     Total $ _____

C. The Difference

Total Income $ _____

Total Monthly Expenses $ _____

Amount over or under what is needed $ _____